First Printed in Great Britain by
Obex Publishing Ltd in 2020

2 4 6 8 10 9 7 5 3 1

This is a work of fiction. Names, characters, businesses, places, events, locales, and incidents are either the products of the author's imagination or used in a fictitious manner. Any resemblance to actual persons, living or dead, or actual events is purely coincidental

Paperback: **978-1-913454-34-0**
eBook: **978-1-913454-35-7**
Hardback: **978-1-913454-36-4**

A CIP catalogue record for this book is available from the British Library.

Obex Publishing Ltd.
Reg. No. 12169917

Little penguin wasn't happy,
as he was always FREEZING.

He shivered every single day,
he didn't find it pleasing.

All he wanted was a blanket,
to keep him nice and warm.

One that he could snuggle in.

Protect him from the storm.

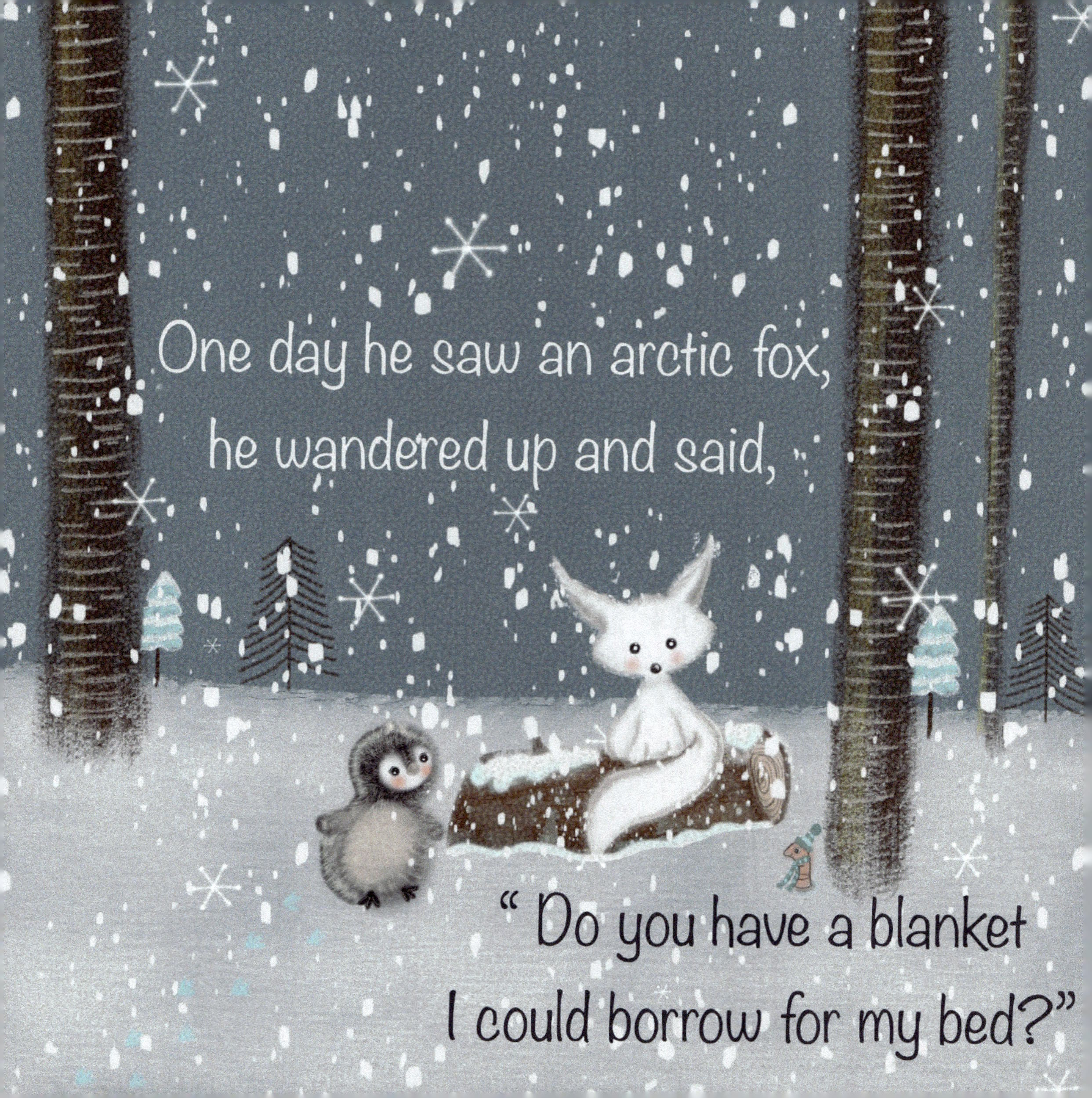

One day he saw an arctic fox,
he wandered up and said,

" Do you have a blanket
I could borrow for my bed?"

"I'm sorry little penguin,
but my coat is nice and thick.

Oh come here for a cuddle
you poor frozen little chick."

Off he went in search of warmth
and found a polar bear.

"Do you have a blanket,
or a jumper I can wear?"

"I'm sorry little penguin,
but I love the snow and ice.
If you are cold the whole
day long,
that really can't be
nice."

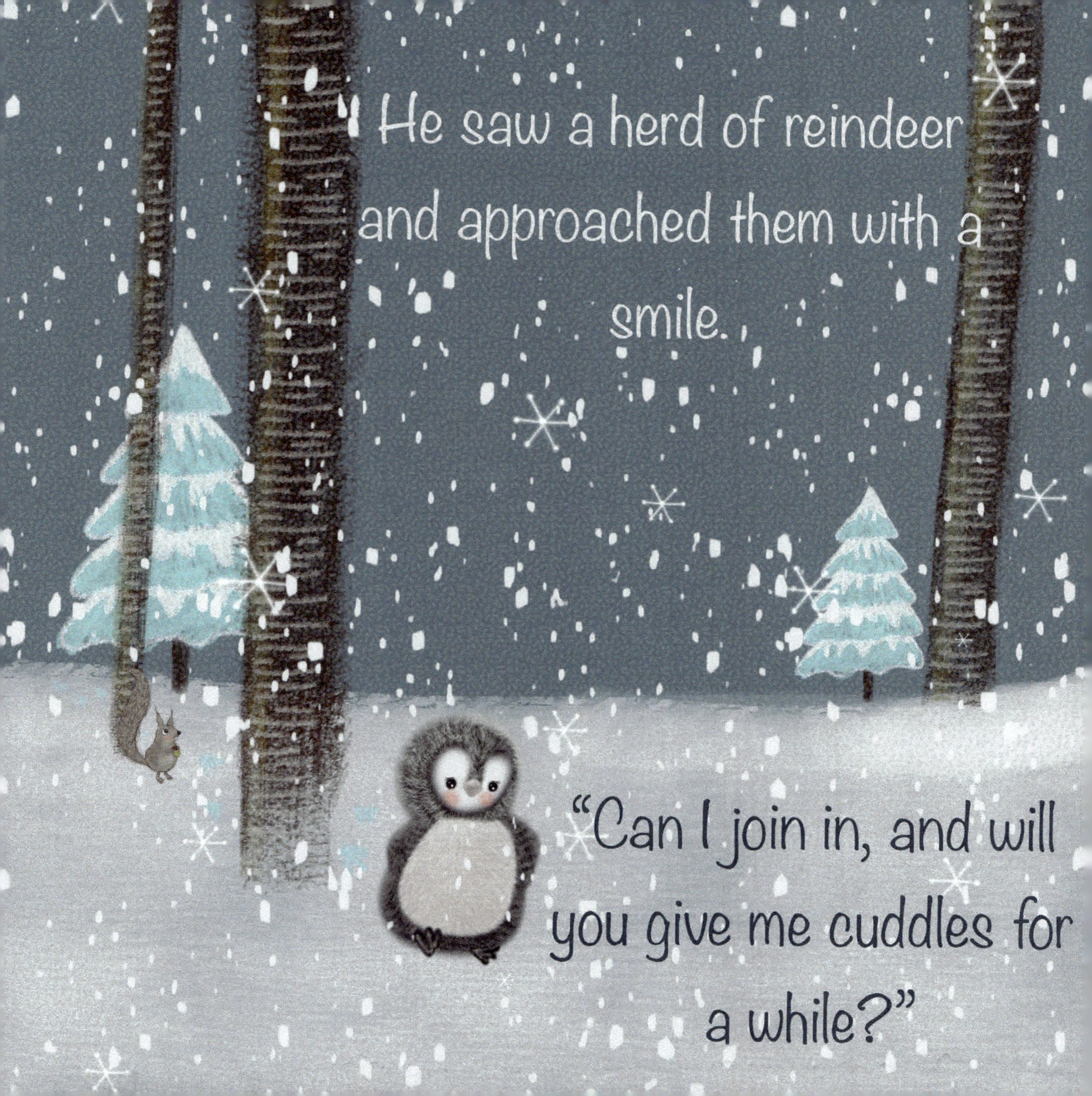

He saw a herd of reindeer and approached them with a smile.

"Can I join in, and will you give me cuddles for a while?"

"You're shivering,
come on snuggle up,"
the mummy reindeer said.

She pulled him in her reindeer arms and
kissed him on the head.

Listening to them talking was
a little arctic hare.

"I wish that I could find you
something nice and warm to wear."

Down then flew a snowy owl,
"What on earths the matter?"

“I’m really cold,” said penguin.
As his teeth began to chatter.

Mrs Snowy took his wing
and cuddled him SO tight.

"Come with me sweet Penguin,
you can stay with me tonight."

She lead him to the family nest,
and told him to climb in.

It was full of feathers

that came right up to his chin

"There's lots of room in here,
now my little owls have flown.
Will you stay with me,
so I can love you as my own?"

"Oh thank you Mrs Snowy,"
Little penguin said.
And soon he started yawning,
he was such a sleepy head.

So penguin lived all cosy,
through the snow and wind and rain.

And in his little feathered nest
was never cold again ...

Lightning Source UK Ltd.
Milton Keynes UK
UKHW051047151121
393986UK00005B/25

9 781913 454340